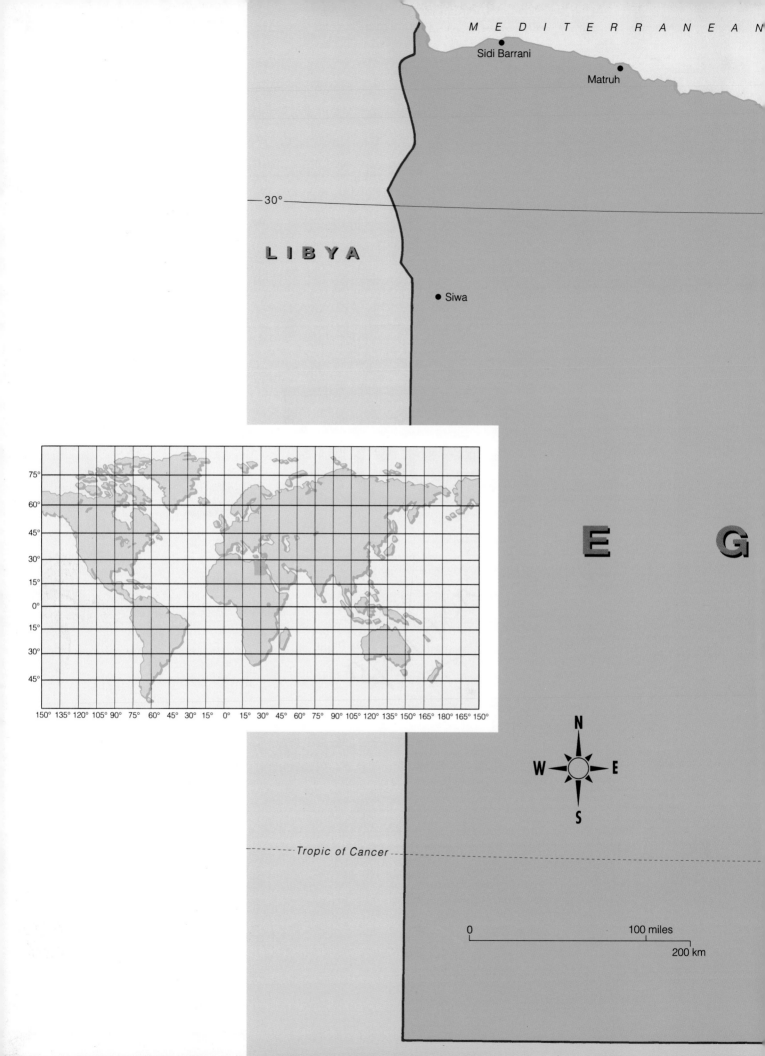

M E D I T E R R A N E A N

Sidi Barrani

Matruh

—30°—

L I B Y A

● Siwa

75°
60°
45°
30°
15°
0°
15°
30°
45°

150° 135° 120° 105° 90° 75° 60° 45° 30° 15° 0° 15° 30° 45° 60° 75° 90° 105° 120° 135° 150° 165° 180° 165° 150°

E   **G**

N
W ● E
S

– – – Tropic of Cancer – – – – – – – – – – – – – –

0   100 miles

200 km

COUNTRY FACT FILES

Egypt

Emma Loveridge

RSVP

RAINTREE
STECK-VAUGHN
PUBLISHERS
The Steck-Vaughn Company

Austin, Texas

Published by Raintree Steck-Vaughn Publishers, an imprint of
Steck-Vaughn Company

Design and typesetting	Roger Kohn Designs
Editor	Diana Russell, Pam Wells
Picture research	Valerie Mulcahy
Illustration	János Márffy
Commissioning editor	Debbie Fox

We are grateful to the following for permission
to reproduce photographs:
Front Cover: Tony Stone Images (C Haigh) *above*, Tony Stone
Images (Hugh Sitton) *below*; Stephanie Colasanti, page 14;
Robert Harding Picture Library, pages 16, 17 (Nigel Francis),
24 (Adam Woolfitt); The Image Bank, pages 8/9 (Kodansha
Images), 30 (Guido Alberto Rossi), 31 and 36 (Infocus
International); Images Of Africa, pages 14/15 (David Keith
Jones); Christine Osborne Pictures, pages 8, 20, 21, 22, 28,
32 and 34 *below*; Planet Earth Pictures, pages 39 (Alain
Dragesco), 40 (Alex Double), 41 (Warren Williams); Rex
Features/Sipa Press, page 43 (Olivier Jobard); Peter Sanders,
pages 34 *above* and 37; Frank Spooner Pictures, page 19
(D Tal); Tony Stone Images, pages 10 (Nigel Press), 27
(Lorentz Gillachsen), 35 (Michael Braid); Sygma, page 42
(F Neema); Travel Ink Photo and Feature Library, pages 23
below and 33 (Abbie Enock); TRIP, pages 11 *left* (R
Crackwell), 11 *right* (C Coe), 25 *above* and *below* (R Tovy),
26 and 29; Marcus Wilson-Smith, page 13; Wind, Sand &
Stars Ltd, pages 12/13, 18, 23 *above*, 38.

The statistics given in this book are the most up to date
available at the time of going to press

Printed in Hong Kong by Wing King Tong

1 2 3 4 5 6 7 8 9 0 HK 99 98 97 96

Library of Congress Cataloging-in-Publication Data
Loveridge, Emma W.
Egypt / Emma Loveridge; (illustration, János Márffy).
p. cm. – (Country fact files)
Includes bibliographical references and index.
Summary: A basic overview of the economy,
geography, and culture of Egypt.
ISBN 0-8172-4626-6
1. Egypt – Juvenile literature. (1. Egypt.) I. Marffy, Janos,
1930- ill. II Title. III. Series.
DT49.L68. 1997
962–dc20
96-33473
CIP AC

CONTENTS

Words that are explained in the glossary are printed in
SMALL CAPITALS the first time they are mentioned in the text.

▬ INTRODUCTION

The borders of the Arab Republic of Egypt are almost identical to those of Egypt in the times of the PHARAOHS. The heart of the country is the Nile Valley and DELTA, where Egyptian civilization emerged more than 5,000 years ago. The great majority of the population today live on just 3 percent of the land along the banks of the Nile River.

The era of the Pharaohs lasted for about 30 centuries, from 3200 B.C. until the conquest of Egypt by the Assyrians in 671 B.C. During this long period, the country was wealthy and powerful, but afterward it was conquered by various other groups or empires. It became Christian when it was part of the Byzantine Empire, but the seventh century A.D. brought the advance of Islam. Gradually, Egypt became Arab-speaking and Muslim, although a significant Coptic Christian minority still remains in the country today.

Egypt was later ruled as part of different European empires, most recently by Great Britain. Independence was declared in 1922, but it was not until 1947 that British troops finally pulled out. The revolution of 1952 that overthrew Egypt's monarchy is seen as the beginning of the country's modern industrial era.

◀ *Many people still have a traditional lifestyle. These women gather together to perform their daily domestic chores.*

▼ Tourism has become the industry that employs more people than any other. There is often a stark contrast between Western-style hotels and facilities for local people.

EGYPT AT A GLANCE

● Area: 386,660 square miles (1,001,450 sq km)
● Population (July 1995 estimate): 62,359,623
● Population density (1995 estimate): 161.3 people per square mile (62.3 people per sq km)
● Capital: Cairo, population estimate 14 million in the metropolitan area
● Other main cities: Alexandria (3,380,000); Port Said (460,000); Suez (388,800)
● Highest mountain: St. Catherine, 8,666 feet (2,642 m)
● Longest river: Nile, 4,145 miles (6,671 km) total, of which 958 miles (1,545 km) are in Egypt
● Language: Arabic
● Religion: Muslim (mostly Sunni) 85%, Christian (mainly Coptic) 15%
● Currency: Egyptian pound, written as E£, divided into 100 piasters
● Economy: Second largest economy (after Saudi Arabia) among Arab countries, based on petroleum products, tourism, the Suez Canal, and agriculture
● Major resources: Oil, natural gas, iron ore, clay, salt, phosphate, gypsum, basalt, dolomite, manganese, lead, zinc
● Environmental problems: Limited freshwater resources, rapid growth in population causing land to be lost to urbanization, desertification, and increased levels of salt in the soil in areas below the Aswan High Dam

Today, Egypt's limited water supply, small amount of agricultural land, and fast-growing population mean that the country has a huge problem just ensuring that its people are fed. However, over the last 25 years Egypt has increased its agricultural yields, improved its industry, raised the general level of its people's health and education, and become a significant power in Middle East politics.

This book gives a wealth of information about the country, from its landscape and climate, to how people in Egypt live today and the future prospects of the country.

THE LANDSCAPE

Egypt covers an area of 386,659 square miles (1 million sq km): approximately three times the size of New Mexico. It is shaped roughly like a square, with a small additional triangular landmass to the east known as the Sinai Peninsula. The country has 1,519 miles (2,450 km) of coastline, which is important for its economic activities since it provides access to the sea, along with fishing and tourist opportunities. Egypt also has borders with Israel, Libya, and Sudan.

Egypt has three main types of landscape: the arid desert regions, the fertile Nile

▲ *This satellite view of the Nile Delta shows the extremely fertile agricultural land around the Nile and the stark contrast of the surrounding desert.*

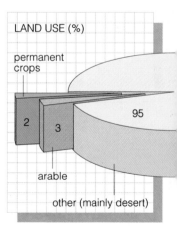

LAND USE (%)

permanent crops

2 3

95

arable

other (mainly desert)

Valley, and small areas of mountains in the south and on the Sinai Peninsula. The desert regions include the Western and Eastern Deserts and the Sinai. Although the desert is vast, there are pockets of OASES, such as Fayyum and Siwa, that provide areas of agriculture and grazing land. There are also smaller water sources, in addition to desert scrubland where the BEDOUIN and BERBER tribes live, grazing their flocks of sheep and goats.

The desert plateau is interrupted by the Nile Valley and Delta. The Nile River flows from the south to the north, providing a fertile area for growing crops. The valley and delta are the most heavily populated areas of Egypt. It is this fertile plain with its supply of fresh water that has shaped the country's history.

The mountains cover a very small area of Egypt. The highest area of land is the granite mountain range of St. Catherine on the Sinai Peninsula. The greatest peak, Mount St. Catherine, stands at 8,666 feet (2,642 m). Covered in snow in the winter, the mountains provide the water source for the Bedouin tribes in the area.

▲ *Inhabited for thousands of years, Luxor stands in a narrow fertile area on the east bank of the Nile. Behind it are the desert mountains.*

◄ *Here in the south Sinai, you can see Nubian sandstone, together with some limestone around the central pink granite mountain range.*

KEY FACTS

● The Nile is the longest river in the world.
● North of Cairo, the Nile divides into 2 branches – the Rosetta and the Damietta.
● 95% of Egypt is made up of desert landscape with less than 2 inches (50 mm) of rain a year.
● The Sinai Peninsula is the only land bridge between Africa and Asia.
● The Nile Valley is at its widest (9.3 miles [15 km]) at Kom Ombo.
● The Qattara Depression is one of the most dangerous areas of desert in the world. Its shifting sands make it extremely difficult to cross.

CLIMATE AND WEATHER

Most of Egypt is very dry. The climate is characterized by a hot season from May to September and a cooler season from November to March. In both seasons, the temperatures are moderated by prevailing north winds.

Most of the little rain that falls in the country is found on the humid Mediterranean coastline, where the average annual rainfall is about 8 inches (200 mm). Away from the sea, this figure falls sharply. Cairo receives an average of around 1.2 inches (30 mm) of rain a year. In Aswan rain is very rare, and in the desert regions there may be a rainstorm only once every few years.

There is an exception to the rule in the mountainous areas of the Sinai Desert, where snow falls every winter. As this slowly melts during the early spring, the local Bedouin collect the water in cisterns to use during the dry summer months.

Wide variations of temperature can occur in the desert regions. Summer daytime temperatures can reach 115°F (46°C), but in the winter, temperatures at night may drop to below freezing.

Between March and May, the hot KHAMSIN winds blow from the south, sometimes

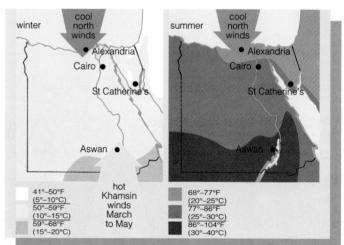

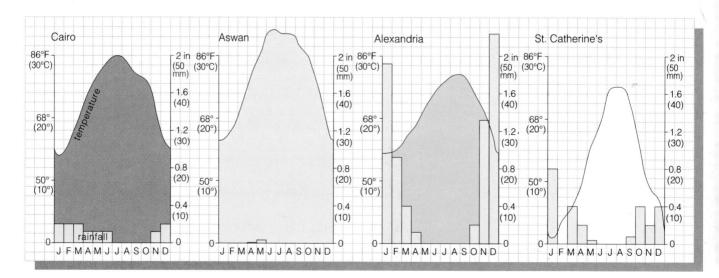

▲ An oasis is a natural water source in a desert area. Oases can range in size from a few square yards to several square miles.

▲ This photograph shows winter snow around St. Catherine's Monastery in the Sinai Peninsula.

KEY FACTS

● In November 1994, severe flooding in UPPER EGYPT killed 580 people and made thousands homeless.
● Sandstorms during the Khamsin can reduce visibility even in central Cairo and disrupt air traffic at the international airport.
● The average rainfall in Egypt is less than 4 inches (100 mm) a year, compared with an average of more than 21.9 inches (555 mm) in Sweden.
● The hottest month is July, with an average daily maximum temperature of 97°F (36°C). The coldest is January, with an average daily minimum temperature of 46°F (8°C).

whipping up the sand and causing sandstorms in the desert. They can also bring rainstorms. When such a storm arrives in Egypt, it causes enormous flash floods. The deluge of water runs straight down the sides of the mountains into the dry riverbeds known as WADIS, creating temporary, but very powerful rivers.

Unfortunately, the country's rainfall is so unpredictable that it cannot be relied upon for agricultural purposes. When the floods do come, they can be totally destructive of anything in their path. This is why the majority of the population live in the Nile Valley and Delta region, using the river's constant supply of fresh water for irrigation. The Nile is relied upon to meet nearly all the country's water needs.

NATURAL RESOURCES

Egypt has a wide variety of mineral deposits. Some of these, such as gold and red granite, have been exploited since ancient times. Today, however, the chief natural resources are oil and gas reserves. These are found mainly in the Gulf of Suez, but also in the Red Sea, the Western Desert near Al-Alamein, on the Nile Delta, and off the north Sinai Mediterranean coastline. Other raw materials produced on a significant scale are iron ore (2.4 million tons a year), phosphate rock (2 million tons) and salt (936,000 tons).

The country is a relatively small producer of oil compared with its Middle East neighbors, producing around 45 million tons of oil a year. But capacity is expected to rise in the coming years, following a decision in 1994 to allow the building of privately owned refineries. At this time, the Gulf of Suez Petroleum Company (GUPCO) is Egypt's largest oil producer, providing approximately 46 percent of the country's total oil output.

Egypt has recently launched a program to build power stations that operate using locally produced natural gas. Gas is also seen as an important potential export. A

◀ *An oil well in the desert. Oil and natural gas have become Egypt's most important natural resources.*

▼ *Hydroelectricity from the Aswan High Dam will produce only 8% of Egypt's electricity by the year 2000, due to fears that another drought will affect supply.*

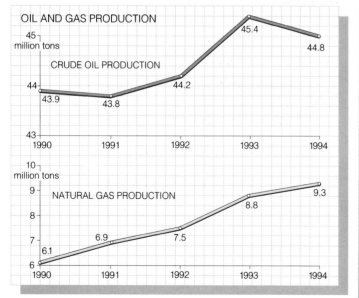

OIL AND GAS PRODUCTION

CRUDE OIL PRODUCTION

	1990	1991	1992	1993	1994
million tons	43.9	43.8	44.2	45.4	44.8

NATURAL GAS PRODUCTION

	1990	1991	1992	1993	1994
million tons	6.1	6.9	7.5	8.8	9.3

KEY FACTS

● Egypt is the second largest producer of refined petroleum products in Africa, following South Africa.

● The phosphate reserves at a massive mine in the Western Desert called Abu Tartur represent about 7% of total world deposits. This mine opened in 1995.

● Two new 60-megawatt wind-power farms are planned in the country.

● The high cost of developing solar power means that it is not a feasible project in Egypt at this time.

● The Aswan High Dam was completed in 1970.

NATURAL RESOURCES

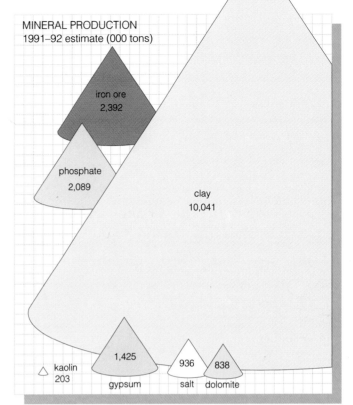

MINERAL PRODUCTION
1991–92 estimate (000 tons)

iron ore 2,392

phosphate 2,089

clay 10,041

kaolin 203

1,425 gypsum

936 salt

838 dolomite

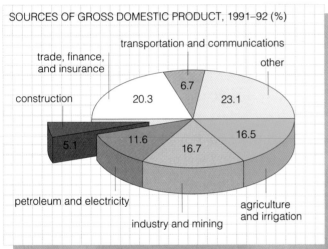

SOURCES OF GROSS DOMESTIC PRODUCT, 1991–92 (%)

transportation and communications

trade, finance, and insurance

other

construction

6.7

20.3

23.1

5.1

11.6

16.7

16.5

petroleum and electricity

industry and mining

agriculture and irrigation

new pipeline carrying gas for export across the Sinai is scheduled to start operations in 1998. One of the main reasons for the new plan is the shortcomings of hydroelectric power. Hydroelectric power from the High Dam at Aswan once supplied 25 percent of Egypt's electricity. However, in 1988 there was a water crisis after eight years of drought in the Nile's catchment areas and a failure in the required supply of electricity from the dam. As a result, Egypt intends to provide 87 percent of its energy capacity from natural gas by the year 2000.

The government is looking at other projects, too. It has an experimental wind-powered plant on the Red Sea coastal area at Zaafarana and has built a submarine cable under the Gulf of Aqaba to Jordan to link the two countries' power grids. Egypt intends to link grids across Africa and the Middle East, to become the central gathering point for regional energy exports to Europe.

POPULATION

◀ *Thebes is a traditional Nile Valley village, where crop and livestock farming form the basis of people's livelihoods.*

▶ *Cairo's central business district. Estimates of the city's population suggest that about one quarter of Egypt's population live in the capital.*

The great majority of Egyptians (about 98 percent) are descended from the indigenous ancient Egyptian population (Hamitic people) or from the Arabs, who conquered the area in the seventh century A.D. A tiny proportion of the population, less than 1 percent, are NUBIANS, who have lived for thousands of years in southern Egypt and northern Sudan along the Nile. There are also some nomadic and seminomadic herders of Arab descent, about 1 percent of the population, called Bedouin, who continue to live in the desert regions.

THE CITIES

Across the country as a whole, the average population density is 161.3 people per square mile (62.3 people per square km). However, the figure is much higher in the cities. In some urban districts, the population density is more than 35,000 people per square mile (100,000 people per square km). This is mainly in slum areas on the outskirts of business districts that have sprung up since the mid-1960s.

Since the late 1970s, the government has tried to encourage industry away from the cities to nonagricultural land. To try to slow the rapid increase in city populations, no new industrial projects are licensed in Cairo or Alexandria. Instead, new industrial sites have been set up in the desert areas around cities — such as southeast of Cairo. There has been no full census in Egypt since 1986, and it is extremely difficult to estimate the expansion of slum areas, but the government believes that this policy has been a factor in reducing the rate at which the cities are growing.

The boom in city populations over the last 30 years has mainly been due to people leaving the countryside in search of work, and also to the overall increase in the country's population. In 1976, there were 33.4 million people in Egypt, compared with more than 60 million today. In other words,

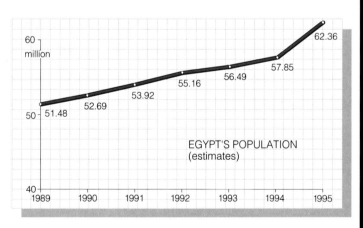

EGYPT'S POPULATION
(estimates)

60 million
62.36
57.85
56.49
55.16
53.92
52.69
51.48
50
40
1989 1990 1991 1992 1993 1994 1995

KEY FACTS

● 49% of people in Egypt live in urban areas.
● 2.5 million Egyptians work outside the country. On average, over the past 20 years 7% of the domestic workforce have found employment abroad.
● An estimated 5 million Sudanese people work in Egypt, providing unskilled labor.
● Arabic is the official language, but a few villages in the Western Desert speak Berber. French and English are widely spoken second languages.
● Part of the Nubians' traditional land was flooded when the Aswan High Dam was built, so many families had to move.
● The country launched its first family-planning project in 1965.
● The earliest Egyptian census dates back to 3340 B.C.

the population has nearly doubled in the last 20 years. However, the rate of increase has started to fall as family planning has been promoted. In 1985, population growth peaked at 3 percent. Today, the figure has dropped to 2.1 percent.

The growth in population is mainly due

◀ *A Bedouin woman and child in traditional clothes, trading bead and metal work. The Bedouin women have their own style of dress. Although they cover their hair and wear veils along with long black cloaks, their handmade dresses can be extremely colorful.*

▶ *Over the last 20 years, Cairo's ancient graveyard, the City of the Dead, has provided shelter for many of the city's poorer inhabitants.*

to improvements in medical facilities. The most important factor is the infant mortality rate. In 1960, there were 179 infant deaths per 1,000 children born; by 1992, there were only 58 per 1,000. Although the size of the average family has fallen by nearly half, to 4.3, today 75 percent more children are reaching adulthood than was the case 30 years ago.

VILLAGE LIFE

About 40 percent of the working population do crop farming or herding. After the revolution in 1952, the government changed the whole pattern of land ownership. Previously, large areas of land were owned by a few wealthy families. The government took over their land and redistributed it to the FELLAHIN, or peasants. But one of the disadvantages with small areas is that the

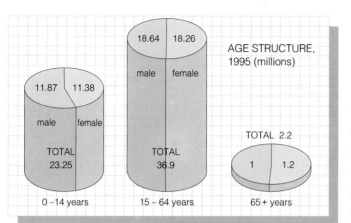

AGE STRUCTURE, 1995 (millions)

18.64 | 18.26
male | female
TOTAL 36.9
15 – 64 years

11.87 | 11.38
male | female
TOTAL 23.25
0 –14 years

TOTAL 2.2
1 | 1.2
65+ years

LIFE EXPECTANCY, 1990–95

	male		female
Egypt	59.2		63.1
U.K.	73.6		78.9
U.S.	72.8		79.9
Turkey	62.5		65.8
India	60.4		61.2

land is used less efficiently and less productively than are larger areas.

DESERT LIFE

The Bedouin still live as nomadic or seminomadic people. Some of them live at the desert oases or by fertile wadis. Families move their homes from season to season with their camels, goats, and sheep so that they use the best grazing and water supplies at any time of the year. They move within certain tribal areas. They also have tribal laws and traditions that are often very different from those in the rest of Egypt. For example, most punishments require a fine to be paid, with the offender handing over a number of goats or camels to the person or family against whom a crime has been committed.

Egypt has faced many difficulties in trying to modernize its industry and ensure that its population is fed. The rapid growth of the population has been the basis of many of today's problems. The country has achieved some of its aims of modernization, but many people are still very poor.

FAMILY LIFE

Three different lifestyles exist side by side. One is the traditional farming way of life in the villages. Around 41 percent (%) of the country's poor live in rural Upper Egypt, although only 29% of the total population live here. Second is the modern, high-technology life of the upper and middle classes in the cities. Nearly 50% of all Egypt's economic establishments are based in the Cairo and Alexandria areas. Third are the families who live in slumlike areas on the outskirts of the large cities. They are drawn there in the hope of finding work. In some cases, the men living here have left their villages in search of work, returning to

▲ *Family life is very important in Egypt, both in the modern cities and in the traditional farming areas along the Nile.*

their families at home about once every month.

Whatever the lifestyle is, the family is extremely important. The extended family, uncles, aunts, grandparents, and so on, gathers to celebrate traditional festivals.

In the modern cities, many women are educated and go out to work. About 4 million women are officially employed, compared with 11 million men. However, in traditional farming areas men and women lead very separate lives. Women usually stay at home to take care of the children

KEY FACTS

● In 1990, it was estimated that 48% of Egyptians over the age of 15 were literate.
● One in four Egyptians is a student or teacher in formal education. The world average is one in five.
● Al-Ahzar University in Cairo was founded in A.D. 970. It first admitted women in 1962.
● The Coptic Church has its own Pope.
● 90% of children are now vaccinated against common childhood diseases.
● 90,000 cases of sickness a year are due to waterborne parasites.

◀ *Egyptian women usually take care of the home. Here, a woman can be seen baking unleavened, or flat, bread. The oven she is using is the traditional dome-shaped "taboon." It is often located on the flat roof of the home.*

COSTS OF SELECTED FOOD AND DRINK ITEMS, 1991–93 (US$)

fresh chicken lb (kg)

Egypt	0.95 (1.89)
Kenya	1.53 (3.06)
Poland	1.05 (2.1)
U.S.	1 (2)
U.K.	3.35 (6.7)
Italy	1.7 (3.4)
Switzerland	4 (8)

flour lb (kg)

Egypt	0.15 (0.3)
Kenya	0.23 (0.46)
Poland	0.2 (0.4)
U.S.	0.25 (0.5)
U.K.	0.3 (0.6)
Italy	0.5 (1)
Switzerland	0.7 (1.4)

potatoes lb (kg)

Egypt	0.19 (0.39)
Kenya	0.12 (0.25)
Poland	0.05 (0.1)
U.S.	0.4 (0.8)
U.K.	0.25 (0.5)
Italy	0.3 (0.6)
Switzerland	0.45 (0.9)

milk quart (liter)

Egypt	(0.33)
Kenya	0.35
Poland	0.3
U.S.	0.7
U.K.	0.9
Italy	1.1
Switzerland	1.2

apples lb (kg)

Egypt	1.35 (2.7)
Kenya	1.7 (3.39)
Poland	0.15 (0.3)
U.S.	0.95 (1.9)
U.K.	0.65 (1.3)
Italy	0.95 (1.9)
Switzerland	1.05 (2.1)

butter lb (kg)

Egypt	0.34 (0.69)
Kenya	0.4 (0.8)
Poland	0.25 (0.5)
U.S.	0.45 (0.9)
U.K.	0.5 (1)
Italy	1 (2)
Switzerland	1.3 (2.6)

sugar lb (kg)

Egypt	0.21 (0.42)
Kenya	0.26 (0.53)
Poland	0.3 (0.6)
U.S.	0.4 (0.8)
U.K.	1.1 (2.2)
Italy	0.55 (1.1)
Switzerland	0.55 (1.1)

and to cook, while the men go to the fields to work or herd the flocks. In the evenings, men usually go out to the local coffee shop. Every town or village has a place where the men relax, talk, and play a game called SHISH BISH. This provides perhaps the most typical scene in Egypt.

Work is not easy to find in Egypt, and unemployment has become high. Out of a labor force of 16 million people, more than 1.5 million are unemployed. However, the rate of unemployment fell from 10.1% to 9.8% between 1992 and 1996 and continues to fall at an even greater rate. Recently, many small cottage industries have flourished, employing both men and women from the towns in activities such as weaving, making shoes, or making pottery.

RELIGION

About 85% of Egyptians are Muslims. There is also a very significant minority of Coptic Christians, plus a tiny percentage of Orthodox Christians, Catholics, and Protestants.

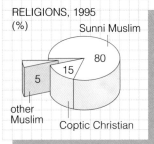

Although *Coptic Christians are in a minority in Egypt, services are held all over the country.*

RELIGIONS, 1995
(%)
Sunni Muslim
80
15
5
other Muslim
Coptic Christian

MUSLIM FESTIVALS AND HOLIDAYS

The Islamic calendar starts from A.D. July 16, 622, when the Prophet Muhammad left Mecca for Medina. The Islamic year has 12 lunar months, which start when the new moon appears, totaling 354 days. Most of the holidays are fixed according to the lunar calendar and, therefore, occur approximately 11 days earlier each year. Friday is the holy day and the day of rest in Egypt.

The major festivals (with dates for 1997) are:

January 11, 1997	BEGINNING OF RAMADAN (a time of fasting)
February 9–12, 1997	ID UL-FITR (the end of Ramadan)
April 9–22, 1997	ID UL-ADHA (related to the Haj, or pilgrimage to Mecca)
May 9, 1997	BEGINNING OF THE MONTH OF MUHARRAM (New Year)
July 18, 1997	BIRTHDAY OF THE PROPHET MUHAMMAD

COPTIC CHRISTIAN (ORTHODOX) FESTIVALS AND HOLIDAYS

Again, the dates of many of these vary. The major festivals (with dates for 1997) are:

January 7, 1997	CHRISTMAS DAY
April 27, 1997	EASTER SUNDAY
June 5, 1997	ASCENSION DAY

Friday is the Muslim holy day, when everything in Egypt closes. On Fridays at noon, the men gather for main prayers in the mosque or other public places. The women usually gather in the home. Muslim prayer is always said facing Mecca, a city in Saudi Arabia that is sacred to Muslims. Many of the Christian churches hold their services on Sunday evenings, rather than mornings, because Sunday is a working day.

Muslims and Christians live side by side. There are laws that restrict certain Christian activities, such as the building of churches, and occasional tensions appear. However, the majority of people are tolerant of each other and work happily together in all areas of business.

EDUCATION

Egypt has both a state education system and a small private system, which educates about 5% of pupils. Over the last 35 years, the government has had great success in raising enrollment rates in schools, colleges,

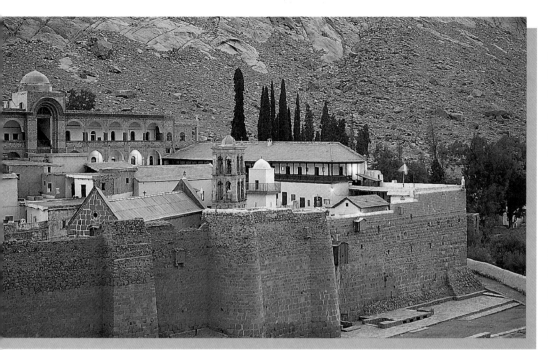

◀ *This church bell tower and minaret stand side by side inside St. Catherine's Monastery in the Sinai Peninsula.*

▼ *Children start school at age 6, but many leave to find work when they reach the age of 12.*

and universities. Elementary education, between the ages of 6 and 12, is compulsory and in some areas it is free, although many children still work rather than attend school. At the age of 12, approximately 1 million children leave school. Those who continue with their education may go to either a general school that prepares students for university or a technical school that

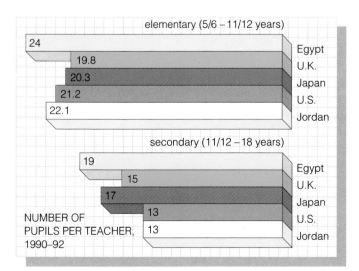

elementary (5/6 – 11/12 years)

24	Egypt
19.8	U.K.
20.3	Japan
21.2	U.S.
22.1	Jordan

secondary (11/12 – 18 years)

19	Egypt
15	U.K.
17	Japan
13	U.S.
13	Jordan

NUMBER OF PUPILS PER TEACHER, 1990–92

specializes in industrial and agricultural subjects. The technical schools train about 25% of the school population.

In 1960, there were only 2.7 million elementary school students, but by 1994 this figure had increased to 8 million. In 1994, 96% of six year olds enrolled for the first year at school. Girls in the rural areas of Upper Egypt are still least likely to be educated.

Egypt has 13 universities, with a total of more than one million students. There are also many technical colleges and institutes of art and music.

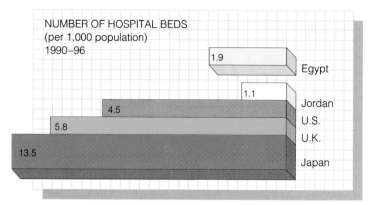

NUMBER OF HOSPITAL BEDS
(per 1,000 population)
1990–96

1.9	Egypt
1.1	Jordan
4.5	U.S.
5.8	U.K.
13.5	Japan

▼ *People sitting and talking in a local coffee shop. This is a common sight everywhere — from modern cities to traditional villages. Most of the customers are men.*

HEALTH

Egypt has made great strides in its health program all over the country. There are private hospitals, and people who can afford it often travel abroad for medical attention. But most of the health institutions are free or charge only a token fee. The rapid population growth, however, has used

up most of the country's resources for health. As a result, the cost of using medical services is now increasing. Most resources are located in the cities, while outlying villages in Upper Egypt and in the slum areas have poor services. Approximately 27% of Egypt's hospital beds are located in central Cairo.

The Bedouin still have traditional tribal doctors. Their medicine is based on the plants and herbs grown in the desert and mountain areas where they live. The government supplies modern clinics in some tribal areas, but the cost of treatment and traditional prejudice tend to mean that they are underused.

◀ *Many farmers along the Nile Valley and in the desert regions earn their living by herding flocks. The shepherds here are from the Luxor area.*

▶ *Carpet-weaving is an industry that commonly employs women, who work for lower wages than men. These girls are employed in a workshop in Cairo.*

RULES AND LAWS

◀ *In Egypt, voting is universal and compulsory for everyone over the age of 18. On election day, there are polling places in every area of the country.*

In 1952, a group of young military officers sent King Farouk into exile, and a new republic was formed under General Neguib. After he died in 1954, Gamal Abdel-Nasser came to power and transformed Egypt politically. His policies included nationalization and the promotion of industrial development. Under Nasser, Egypt also fought two major wars against Israel, in 1956 and 1967. Under his successor, Anwar Sadat, Egypt fought another war against the Israeli occupation of Sinai. In 1973, this resulted in the Camp David Accords. These provided the basis for a peace treaty between Egypt and Israel, signed in Washington, D.C., in 1979. Sadat was assassinated in 1981 by those who opposed the peace with Israel. He was succeeded by Hosni Mubarak.

Egypt's head of state is the president of the republic, who is nominated by a two-thirds majority of the Majlis al-Shaab (People's Assembly) and elected by

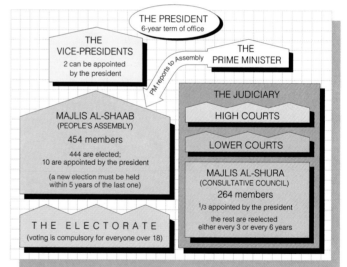

referendum. The president enjoys vast powers and is also supreme commander of the armed forces.

The People's Assembly has 444 directly elected members, with ten extra members chosen by the president. The prime minister reports to the assembly, but decisions are ultimately made by the president, in

KEY FACTS

- In 1995, there were two Bedouin members of the People's Assembly.
- There are 12 recognized opposition parties to the ruling National Democratic Party.
- Egypt sent 32,000 troops to the Persian Gulf to fight against Iraq in 1991. This was the second largest group of foreign troops, after the one sent by the U.S.
- Egypt has 440,000 active armed forces members. More than half of these are drafted, or obliged to serve in the armed forces for a period of time.
- If a family has only one son, he does not have to serve as draftee.

consultation with ministers and advisers. The ruling National Democratic Party (NDP) was last elected in 1995 and has held a clear majority since it was founded in 1978. The main opposition party is the New Wafd.

Egypt has been one of the most prominent countries in the Arab world. In 1990–1991, it played a key role in an Arab coalition to oppose Iraq's invasion and annexation of Kuwait.

▼ *President Anwar Sadat's memorial was built after his assassination in 1981. He was assassinated by the Islamic Jihad.*

FOOD AND FARMING

There are an estimated 3.5 million farmers cultivating small holdings along the Nile Delta or Valley. The yields from these farms are among the highest per acre in the world. The major crops are cotton, rice, corn, wheat, clover, and beans. Sugarcane is also important in Upper Egypt, covering about 15 percent of the arable land. Enough fruit and vegetable crops are grown to allow the surplus to be exported.

One of the main problems that prevents further increases in output is the insufficient supply of water. The farmers depend entirely on the Nile River and on irrigation. Only 2 percent of the cultivated land is irrigated by modern methods. These methods allow for watering in selected areas rather than flooding the whole area and wasting water. Irrigation water is

▲ *A traditional form of irrigating the land. The donkey turns the wheel, scooping water into hand-dug irrigation channels that crisscross the land.*

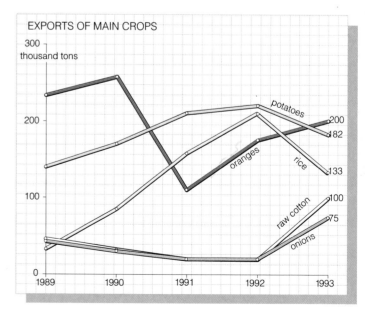

EXPORTS OF MAIN CROPS

300 thousand tons

potatoes 200
182
oranges
rice
133
raw cotton 100
75
onions

200

100

0

1989   1990   1991   1992   1993

provided free of charge by the government. The other problem is waterlogging in the fields. Only one-third of the agricultural land is serviced by drains. Many are old and need repair. There is not sufficient drainage to counterbalance the high level of salt in the soil.

Every year, 1,037,800 acres (420,000 ha) of desert are reclaimed by the government to become cultivable land. This involves either extending existing areas of irrigation, or piping water to desert areas that can then operate a new irrigation system. Nevertheless, the overall amount of agricultural land has not increased. This is because an equal amount of farmland is lost every year to urbanization, when more houses and other facilities are built on the outskirts of towns and cities to accommodate the country's growing population.

Although crop production has grown by 2.5 percent over the last decade, despite the many water problems, production of livestock has fallen significantly since 1990. Many of the ups and downs are related to the payment of government subsidies (allowances) to farmers. Sharp fluctuations in production and in the prices of water buffalo and poultry have put many farmers out of business.

▼ *Watermelons are grown chiefly in the Nile Delta region. They ripen in late spring or early summer and are then taken to the market.*

EGYPT'S FISHING CATCH (live weight)

	1990	1991	1992
total catch	313	299.9	287.1
freshwater fish	237.7	216.3	206.3
marine fish	75.3	83.6	80.8

thousand tons

▼ *The government is encouraging fishing in the Bitter Lakes, to try to help increase the annual catch.*

Egypt has an important fishing industry. The total catch amounts to approximately 300,000 tons a year. Less than one-third comes from the open sea. The most productive fishing areas are the shallow lakes in the Nile Delta, Birket Qarun, and the Red Sea. A fishing industry is also being developed in Lake Nasser, the lake formed by the building of the Aswan High Dam. The government is hoping to double the fish catch by the year 2000. It is encouraging people to make greater use of the country's inland lakes and waterways.

There are still a few traditional Bedouin fishing villages on the east coast of Sinai. For centuries, the Bedouin have fished on the coral reef flats of the Red Sea, but more recently increased demand and national

◀ *Most families use spices in their daily cooking. They are sold both in modern supermarkets and in traditional spice stores.*

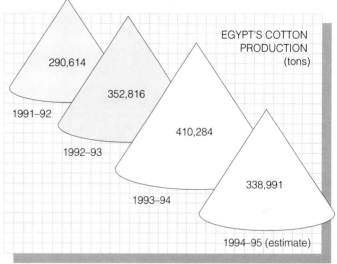

EGYPT'S COTTON PRODUCTION (tons)

290,614 — 1991–92

352,816 — 1992–93

410,284 — 1993–94

338,991 — 1994–95 (estimate)

park subsidies have changed the pattern of fisheries in the area. Instead of just catching enough fish to eat, the Bedouin have increased their catch so that they can sell the surplus.

Rice, potatoes, bread, and vegetables are the staple diet in most Egyptian households. They are usually very lightly spiced. Cumin is the most common spice used. Almost all meals are eaten with flat, unleavened bread. Meals are usually eaten communally, with the family sharing the food laid out on plates placed on a central low table. Sometimes the meal will begin with several small dishes of tahini (made from sesame seeds), hummus, yogurt, and mashed, spiced eggplant.

The diet of wealthier families is similar to that in Western countries. Most of the poultry and meat that they eat is boiled, and the vegetable comes as a form of sauce to be poured over the rice that is part of most meals. A beef, or lamb kabob, or a

KEY FACTS

● Egyptian farmers have used artificial fertilizers since 1902, when completion of the first Aswan Dam meant they could no longer use the natural fertilizers in silt from the Nile.

● Egypt is the world's most important producer of long-staple (long-fibered) cotton, which is very high quality.

● The sardine fisheries along the Mediterranean coast have been greatly depleted since the construction of the Aswan High Dam.

● The limits on Egypt's arable land and its rapidly growing population have pushed up food imports to 60% of food consumption.

● Egyptians are recommended to eat cucumbers in large numbers in the summer, to help prevent dehydration and resulting sickness in the heat.

● Cairo's first McDonald's Restaurant opened in 1995.

chicken, pigeon, or fish dish is commonly the key part of the main meal.

Egypt has a traditional dessert called "umm ali" that is very similar to rice pudding. There is also a large variety of desserts made from pastry, sesame seeds, nuts, and honey. Large quantities of these are made at festivals or holidays and are shared with family, friends, and neighbors.

The diet of the desert people is different from that in the Nile Valley. Food is very sparse in the desert, and the nomads usually live on bread, sweet tea, and dates.

MAIN AGRICULTURAL AREAS

- cotton, rice, wheat, and fruit
- sugarcane, fruit, vegetables, and livestock
- fishing

If the rain comes and the goat herds produce plenty of milk, then the families will make cheese. The Bedouin very rarely eat meat, but on a festival day they will take a goat from the herd and cook it over a wood fire in the desert. On the feast of Id ul-Fitr, at the end of the fast of Ramadan, the leaders of the tribe and those families who have large herds will slaughter enough goats for the poorer members of the tribe to share the feast.

◄ *Many rural families breed baby pigeons for sale and to supplement the family diet. Here, eggs are being collected from pigeon houses, which are traditionally made of mud or clay.*

TRADE AND INDUSTRY

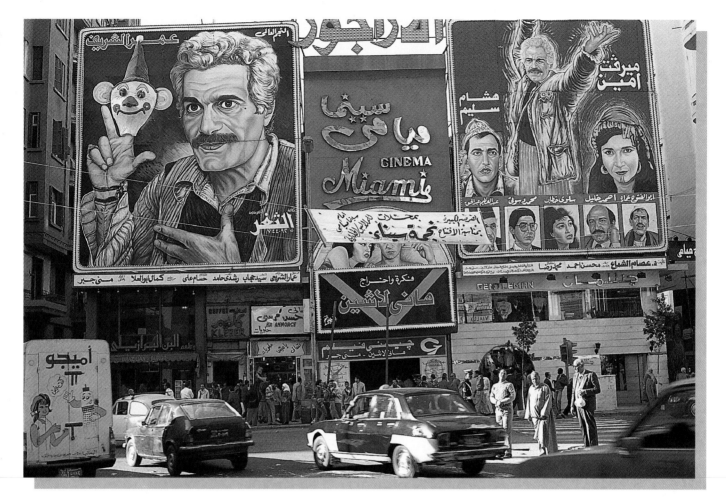

INDUSTRIAL EXPANSION

Since 1952, the government has assigned top priority to industrial expansion. In 1965, total industrial production was US$ 2.71 billion annually. Twenty years later, output exceeded US$ 13 billion a year. In addition to the oil trade and cotton textile trade, other important industries are the manufacture of cement, refined sugar, fertilizers, tires and inner tubes, television receivers, iron, and steel. Since 1991, Egypt has also begun to assemble motor vehicles in cooperative projects with foreign manufacturers.

The Suez Canal provides the shortest ocean route from Europe to Asia. Each of the 17,500 ships using the canal every year is charged a fee for passing through it. This trade has helped to expand the revenues

▲ *Egypt's films and film stars are popular all over the Arab world.*

received by the country since the canal was reopened in 1975.

Egypt is also trying to compete in the world information technology market, using the large local pool of cheap skilled labor in the same way as other developing countries, such as India and Singapore, have done. Egypt now earns US$ 172 million from software production. It is predicted that this sector will grow at 35 percent a year until 1998, compared with the global rate of 9–15 percent.

PRIVATIZATION

Private industry and trade have recently become more and more important.

Privatization is a slow and controversial process, but small firms employing perhaps ten workers are adding significantly to the job pool and to revenue. The tourism and car assembly industries are now dominated by the private sector, although other areas are likely to follow more slowly. At present, the private sector accounts for 50 percent of non-oil exports and 25 percent of imports.

TOURISM AND FILMMAKING

Tourism is Egypt's main source of foreign exchange. Directly and indirectly, it provides one in ten jobs. Despite problems with the poor availability of services, such as roads, it remains the top money earner, bringing in revenues of US$ 2–3 billion a year.

Egypt has traditionally relied on its archaeological heritage to attract tourists. Sites such as the Pyramids and the Sphinx at Giza are unique. Today, new attractions revolve around the sun and sea, particularly scuba-diving vacations and safaris. Major expansion has been centered on Hurghada and Sharm al-Sheikh on the Red Sea coast.

KEY FACTS

● Pyramids Technology Valley is a new center being developed to give Egypt a share in the growing international information technology market.
● The Suez Canal was closed from 1967 to 1975.
● Egypt has a fairly large defense industry, employing 75,000 of the highest-paid workers. It produces both armaments and various industrial goods for use within the civilian sector.
● The number of hotel rooms in Egypt has more than doubled to 60,000 in the last ten years. It is expected to double again in the next ten years.

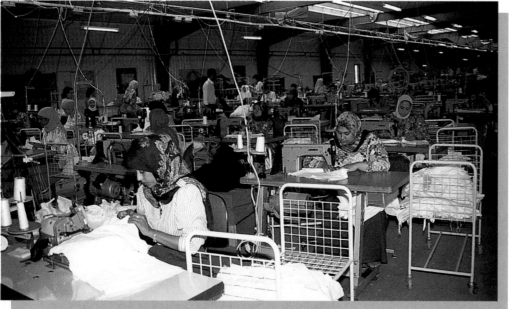

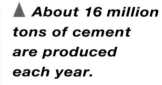

▲ *About 16 million tons of cement are produced each year.*

◀ *The state-owned textile industry suffers from outdated technology and quality control. But 90 percent of the ready-made garment industry is in private hands.*

Egypt is the main filmmaking country in the Arab world. It has a state-operated cinema corporation and numerous private film companies. Although there are many dialects of Arabic throughout the Arab-speaking world, the Egyptian dialect is the most universally understood, because of the widespread distribution and viewing of Egyptian films.

▲ *The temples at Abu Simbel are among the great ancient Egyptian sites visited by hundreds of thousands of tourists every year.*

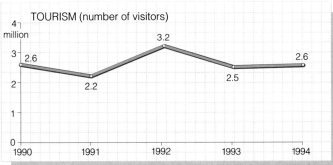

TOURISM (number of visitors)

4 million
3 — 2.6
2.2
3.2
2.5
2.6
2 —
1 —
0
1990   1991   1992   1993   1994

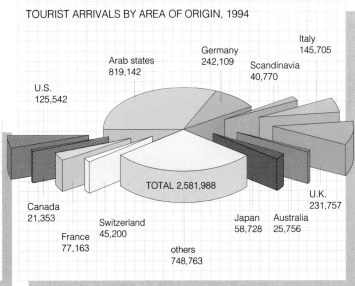

TOURIST ARRIVALS BY AREA OF ORIGIN, 1994

U.S. 125,542
Arab states 819,142
Germany 242,109
Scandinavia 40,770
Italy 145,705

TOTAL 2,581,988

Canada 21,353
France 77,163
Switzerland 45,200
others 748,763
Japan 58,728
Australia 25,756
U.K. 231,757

TRANSPORTATION

One in every 12 families in Egypt owns a car and at least 50 percent of these families are located in the Cairo, Giza, and Alexandria city areas. The number of people owning cars is rising. The main highways connect Cairo with Alexandria, Port Said, Suez, and Al-Fayyum.

The Egyptian government estimates that approximately ten million people in the country use public transportation every day. Public buses are available between Egyptian cities and villages, but they tend to be old and in poor condition.

Egypt's railroad system is one of the oldest in the Middle East. More than one-third of its 3,100 miles (5,000 km) of track was built before the opening of the Suez Canal in 1869. The government has now begun a badly needed modernization program. The Egyptian National Railroads provide cheap travel for people, since the railroads receive government subsidies of about 50 percent. The principal line links Aswan to towns along the Nile Valley and to Alexandria on the Mediterranean Seacoast.

The central area of Cairo has an underground train system. It was extended in 1987 and work began in 1993 on a second line into Giza. Currently, more than 1 million people use this system to travel to work, and 5 million are expected to use it when the new line is completed in 1998.

The country has a large network of airports. About 80 are used for Egyptian business and for tourism. The national airline is Egyptair, which runs both

▼ *Because of high import taxes on vehicles, many of Egypt's cars are very old. Almost all taxis date from the 1970s.*

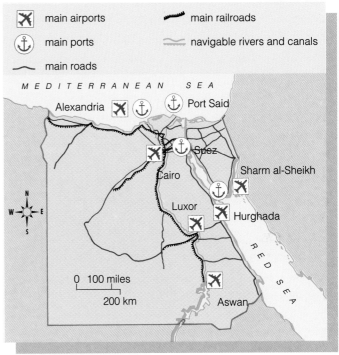

◀ *The ferry at Luxor is one of many along the Nile Valley and the irrigation canals. It is used to transport laborers to work.*

✈ main airports ⌇ main railroads

⚓ main ports ≈ navigable rivers and canals

— main roads

MEDITERRANEAN SEA

Alexandria ✈ ⚓   ⚓ Port Said

✈ ⚓ Suez

Cairo   Sharm al-Sheikh ⚓ ✈

Luxor ✈ Hurghada

RED SEA

0 100 miles
200 km   Aswan ✈

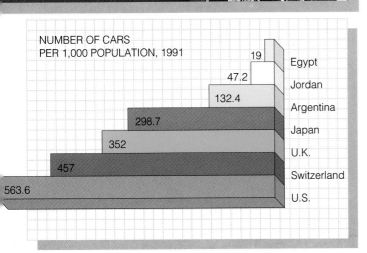

NUMBER OF CARS
PER 1,000 POPULATION, 1991

19	Egypt
47.2	Jordan
132.4	Argentina
298.7	Japan
352	U.K.
457	Switzerland
563.6	U.S.

international and domestic flights. Cairo has become an important hub for air traffic in the Middle East. However, Egyptair imposes severe restrictions on foreign charter flights to the capital. New terminals and extensions are planned for Cairo and for Nuweiba, which is a growing center in Sinai on the Gulf of Aqaba.

Alexandria is the main port and handles one-third of Egypt's international trade. Port Said and Suez are the second and third largest ports, but congestion is forcing the government to look to expand others as alternatives. The inland waterways are important for trading routes and for the movement of people looking for work. There are 1,922 miles (3,100 km) of navigable waterways, including the Nile River. Some of these are irrigation canals that are used for transportation in the Nile Delta. These canals are important for the economy and are used extensively.

Since 1977, the Suez-Mediterranean (SUMED) pipeline has provided an alternate route to the Suez Canal for oil transported between the Red Sea and the Mediterranean. Egypt owns 50 percent of the shares in this pipeline, with the rest owned by Abu Dhabi, Saudi Arabia, and Kuwait. Egypt also has an extensive network of oil product pipelines that are used for the domestic distribution and transportation of crude oil. These pipelines supply refineries and reach export terminals.

▼ *Modern catamarans on the Red Sea have recently become a popular way for tourists to travel.*

KEY FACTS

● The Cairo metro (subway) is one of the most intensively used systems in the world.
● Camel caravans are still used to a limited extent in the desert regions.
● Alexandria has the largest water area of any Mediterranean harbor.
● Work is in progress to deepen the Suez Canal by about 3.9 feet (1.2 m). At present, only ships that need a depth of less than 54.9 feet (16.75 m) can pass through. Some modern tankers need a much greater depth and, therefore, cannot pass.

THE ENVIRONMENT

Egypt has only recently begun to take steps to prevent its environment from being heavily damaged by industry. In 1992, with assistance from the World Bank, the government brought in an environmental action plan, and in 1994 it gave greater powers to the Egyptian Environmental Affairs Agency. This body deals with issues relating to clean air, the marine environment, and hazardous waste. It also acts as an inspection agency, ensuring that industries follow the environmental laws.

One of Egypt's biggest environmental problems is industrial waste. It is estimated that Egyptian industries dump about 10 tons of solid waste every minute (a third of which is uncontrolled) on canal banks or in landfills and drains. Fines are imposed on industries who break the environmental laws.

The establishment of national parks has been another important development in Egypt. The most famous is Ras Muhammad Marine National Park in south Sinai. This was defined as a "protected area" in 1983 and classified as a national park in 1989. It was established in order to protect the coral reef against the dangers of sewage and pollution from the growing towns and industry, and from the effects of tourism and shipping. Enormous damage can be caused to the coral if ships run into it. For example, a cruise ship ran aground on the Red Sea

▲ *The Dorcas gazelle is specially adapted to the desert. It absorbs all the water it needs from the plants it eats.*

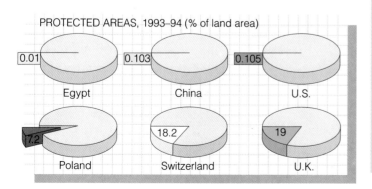

PROTECTED AREAS, 1993–94 (% of land area)

0.01	0.103	0.105
Egypt	China	U.S.
7.2	18.2	19
Poland	Switzerland	U.K.

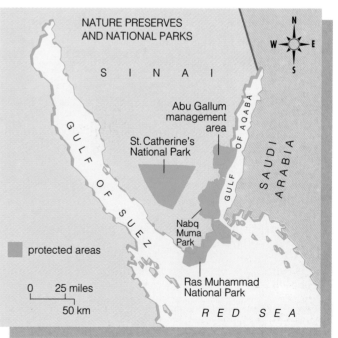

NATURE PRESERVES AND NATIONAL PARKS

S I N A I

GULF OF SUEZ

GULF OF AQABA

GULF

SAUDI ARABIA

Abu Gallum management area

St. Catherine's National Park

Nabq Muma Park

protected areas

Ras Muhammad National Park

0   25 miles
50 km

R E D   S E A

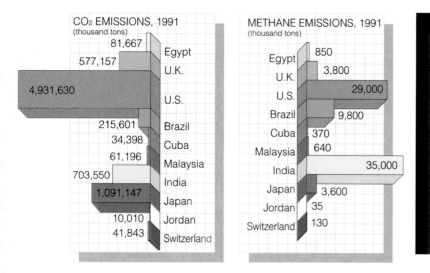

CO₂ EMISSIONS, 1991
(thousand tons)

81,667	Egypt
577,157	U.K.
4,931,630	U.S.
215,601	Brazil
34,398	Cuba
61,196	Malaysia
703,550	India
1,091,147	Japan
10,010	Jordan
41,843	Switzerland

METHANE EMISSIONS, 1991
(thousand tons)

Egypt	850
U.K.	3,800
U.S.	29,000
Brazil	9,800
Cuba	370
Malaysia	640
India	35,000
Japan	3,600
Jordan	35
Switzerland	130

KEY FACTS

● Cairo's air contains the highest levels of lead in the world.
● Falconry and the hunting of endangered species have been banned since 1994.
● The country has 16 national parks under the control of the Egyptian Environmental Affairs Agency, which is answerable directly to the prime minister.

coral reef in 1996 and caused great harm.

The marine national park covers some of the world's most beautiful and varied coral and fish life. Its establishment has made a good impact on the area. Hotels in the Sharm al-Sheikh area on the edge of the national park must now meet the sewage, drainage, and anchoring restrictions laid down by the park. They are also charged a small fee for each night a tourist stays with them. Payment of these fees goes toward the upkeep of the park and the employment of rangers to monitor the plan.

The newest national park includes the St. Catherine's Mountain Range in the center of south Sinai. The desert and mountains of this region contain rare archaeological sites. They are also the home of many species of animal, insect, and plant life. Sinai is relatively isolated, and, therefore, many of the life forms here are unique.

◀ **Some coastal areas are at risk from oil pollution and are also littered with trash, such as plastic containers and tin cans.**

▶ **The Red Sea coral reef is one of the world's most beautiful reefs. The marine national park now aims to protect it from damage.**

THE FUTURE

E gypt has achieved a great deal in addressing the problems of a country with a tiny area of farmland, limited natural water resources, and the different lifestyles of its people, ranging from those with well-paid jobs in the cities to those who are traditional villagers.

Over the last 30 years, the country has made great advances in changing the structure of the economy and improving the living standards of its people. Enrollment in schools has grown, health conditions have improved, and life expectancy has increased. The government hopes these trends will continue.

Egypt will play an important role in any future peace agreements that may be reached in the Middle East. There have

KEY FACTS

● Egypt's population is expected to reach 76.6 million in the year 2007.
● The population of Cairo is expected to reach 16 million by the year 2000.
● Further peace talks for the Middle East are planned, using Egypt as a neutral base and a negotiator.
● Egypt is upgrading its transportation links by building a bridge across the Suez Canal at Ferdan. It is due to be completed in 1998.
● Further expansion of the private sector could mean that highly qualified Egyptians working outside the country may find jobs at home instead.

◀ *After restoration, the tomb of Queen Nefertari reopened to the public in 1995. This marked the beginning of a major restoration program backed by the government and international community. The aim is to use modern techniques to protect ancient sites.*

▲ *Sharm al-Sheikh provided the center for the Middle East peace conference held on March 13, 1996. Various world leaders, including Egypt's president, were involved in trying to advance the peace process between Israel and its other Arab neighbors.*

been very difficult times for the region in the last 40 years, most recently with the Gulf War of 1991. However, since the peace treaty between Egypt and Israel was signed in 1979, there has been greater political stability in the country, which has benefited trade. Peace in the area as a whole would allow the development of large regional projects, including plans to make more productive use of the most precious and most needed natural resource — water. Moreover, Egypt is hoping to forge a trade agreement in the Middle East that would

involve links between 100 million people in the area by the year 2000.

If its economy grows and peace is achieved, Egypt's prospects in the next century look bright. It has many natural resources, including oil and gas, and a large and mostly young workforce. It also occupies a key geographical position, which will allow the country to become the central link for trade, particularly energy resources, across the Middle East area, from the Red Sea to the Mediterranean and from Asia to Europe.

FURTHER INFORMATION

● EGYPTIAN TOURIST AUTHORITY
630 Fifth Avenue, New York, NY 10111
*Provides leaflets, maps, and general
information on Egypt.*

● EGYPTIAN EMBASSY
352 International Court, N.W.
Washington, D.C. 20008
*Provides help with general questions
on Egypt.*

● EGYPTAIR
720 Fifth Avenue, New York, NY 10019

● EGYPTIAN TRAVEL SERVICE
4353 N. Harding Avenue, Chicago, IL 60618

BOOKS ABOUT EGYPT

Balkwill, Richard. *Food and Feasts in
Ancient Egypt.* Macmillan, 1994

Cross, Wilbur. *Egypt.* Children's Press, 1982

DeBruycker, Daniel and M. Dauber. *Egypt
and the Middle East.* Barron, 1995

Department of Geography. *Egypt in Pictures.*
Lerner, 1988.

Ganeri, Anita. *Egyptians.* Watts, 1993

Harrison, Steve and Patricia. *Egypt.*
Parkwest, 1992

Morrison, Ian A. *Egypt.* Raintree Steck-
Vaughn, 1991

Pateman, Robert. *Egypt.* Marshall
Cavendish, 1992

GLOSSARY

BEDOUIN
The tribal people of Arabia. They make up
about 1 percent of the population of Egypt,
living in Sinai and the Western and Eastern
deserts.

BERBERS
A tribal people of North Africa. A very small
number live in the outer oases of the
Western Desert in Egypt.

DELTA
The triangular-shaped area at the mouth of
a river, where it divides into many small
branches flowing into the sea.

FELLAHIN
The poorer peasants in the Nile Valley area.

KHAMSIN
The hot winds that blow across Egypt
between March and May, causing sandstorms.
They are also called the Simoon.

NUBIANS
A people who live in the south of Egypt and
the north of Sudan.

OASIS
An area in the desert where water is forced
to the surface for geological reasons and
that provides a source of fresh water.

PHARAOH
The term used in ancient Egypt to refer to
the king.

SHISH BISH
A popular game in Egypt. It is played by
two people, using a backgammon board.

UPPER EGYPT
The name given to the south of Egypt,
where the upper part of the Egyptian Nile
flows from the south toward the north.

WADI
A dry riverbed that may suddenly fill
with water after a rainstorm.

© Macdonald
Young Books 1996

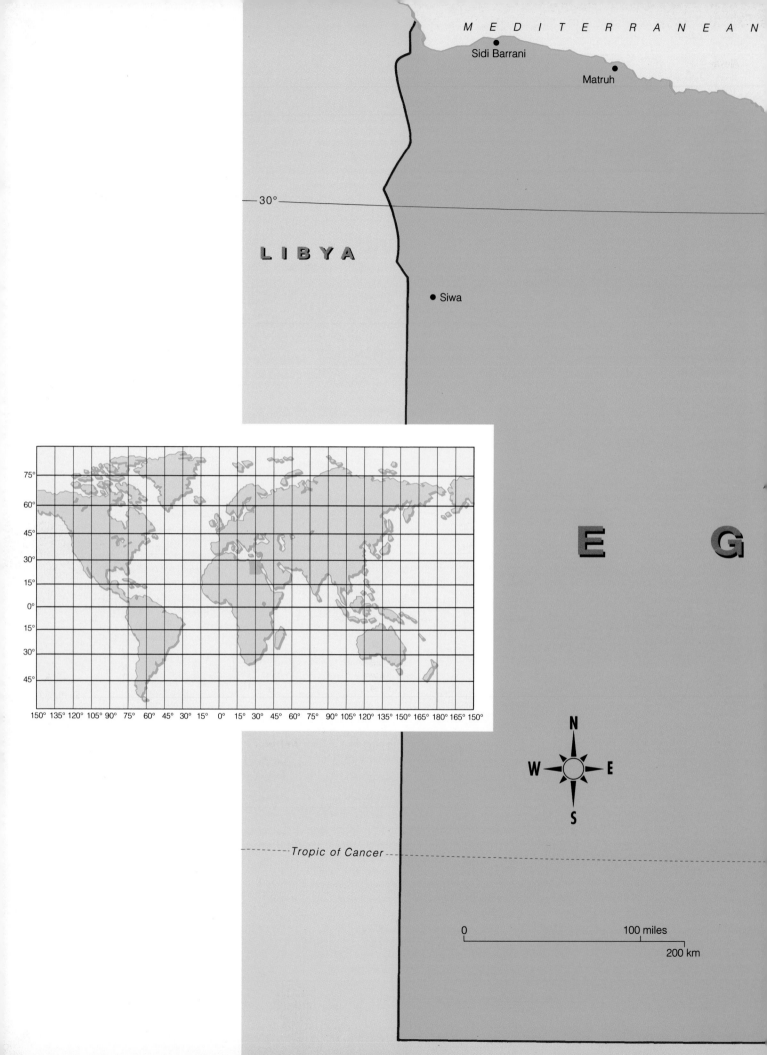

M E D I T E R R A N E A N

● Sidi Barrani

Matruh ●

—30°—

L I B Y A

● Siwa

E   G

75°
60°
45°
30°
15°
0°
15°
30°
45°

150° 135° 120° 105° 90° 75° 60° 45° 30° 15° 0° 15° 30° 45° 60° 75° 90° 105° 120° 135° 150° 165° 180° 165° 150°

N

W ◆ E

S

Tropic of Cancer

0   100 miles

200 km

● Sidi Barrani

Loveridge, Emma

Egypt

$24.25

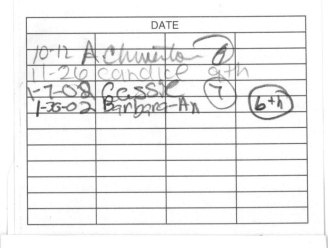

DATE			
10-12 A Chrisler ...			
11-26 candice 9th			
1-7-08 Cassie		7	
1-30-02 Barbara-An			6+1

Egypt (Country Fact Files)

Emma Loveridge
AR B.L.: 8.1
Points: 1.0   962